THIS IS A BORZOI BOOK PUBLISHED BY ALFRED A. KNOPF

Copyright © 2020 by Lizzy Rockwell All rights reserved. Published in the United States by Alfred A. Knopf,

an imprint of Random House Children's Books, a division of Penguin Random House LLC, New York.

Knopf, Borzoi Books, and the colophon are registered trademarks of Penguin Random House LLC.

Visit us on the Web! rhcbooks.com   Educators and librarians, for a variety of teaching tools,

visit us at RHTeachersLibrarians.com

Library of Congress Cataloging-in-Publication Data is available upon request.

ISBN 978-0-375-82204-9 (trade) — ISBN 978-0-375-92204-6 (lib. bdg.) — ISBN 978-0-375-98751-9 (ebook)

The illustrations in this book were created using watercolor, ink, and scans of fabric.

Book design by Sarah Hokanson

MANUFACTURED IN CHINA   October 2020 10 9 8 7 6 5 4 3 2 1 First Edition

Random House Children's Books supports the First Amendment and celebrates the right to read.

Dedicated, with love,
to the quilters at Peace by Piece:
The Norwalk Community
Quilt Project

The All-Together Quilt

Lizzy Rockwell

Alfred A. Knopf
New York

Jennifer and her friends
meet on Fridays at the
community center.
They are making a quilt.
Everyone works together.

First, Jennifer picks a fabric
from the dark colors.

Fran picks a fabric
from the light colors.

Jennifer traces
a shape on the
dark fabric.
Then she traces
a shape on the
light fabric.

Fran cuts out
two shapes.

Jennifer pins them together.

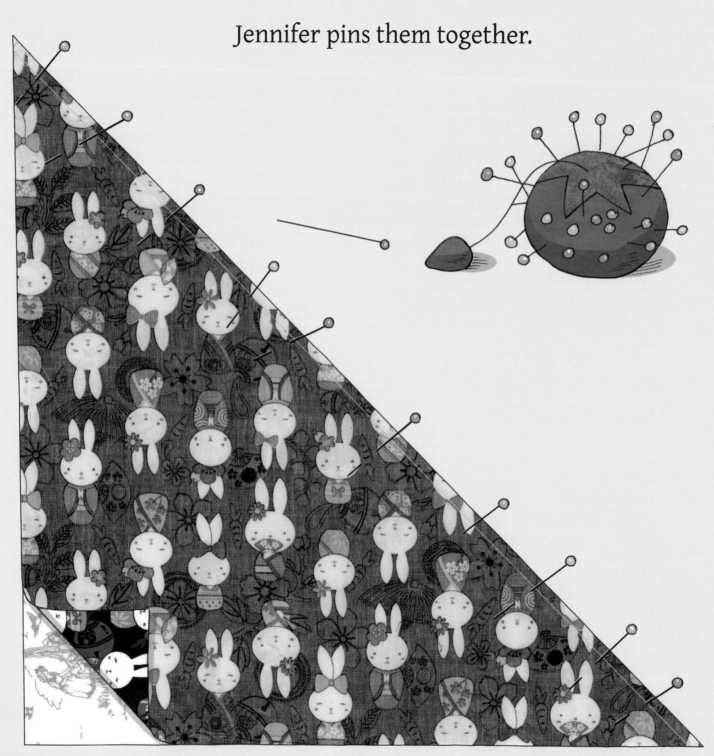

Right sides face each other.

Fran sews them together.

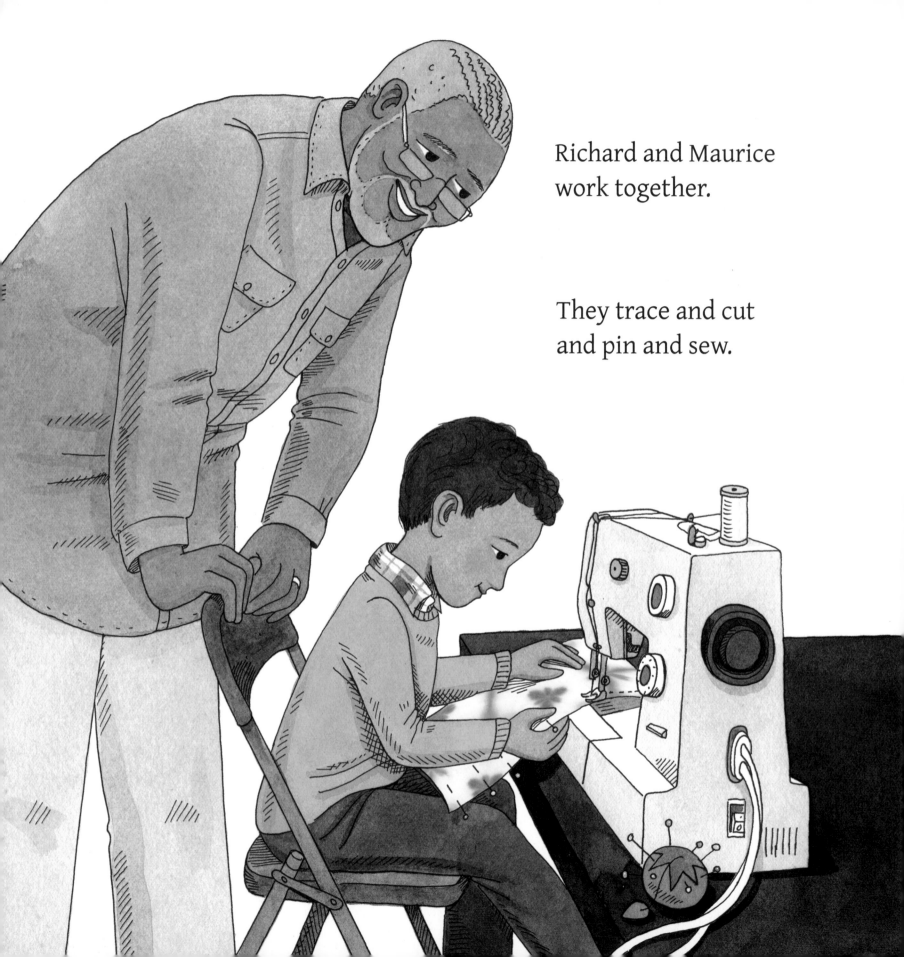

Richard and Maurice
work together.

They trace and cut
and pin and sew.

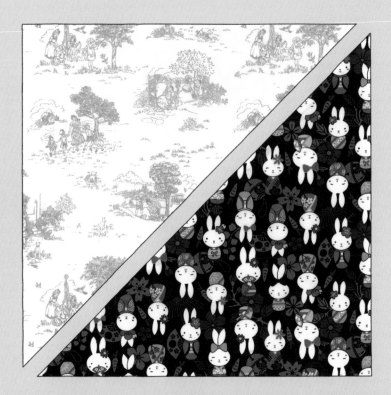

Look! Two triangles together make one square.

Two rectangles together make one square.

Fran and
Jennifer

Richard and
Maurice

Sanaa and
Malissa

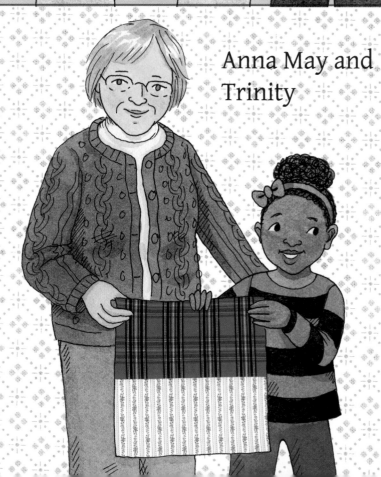

Anna May and
Trinity

Maria and Jocelyn

Nadelin and Viola

Angela and Betty

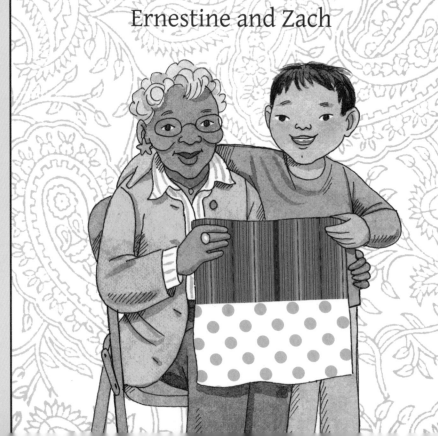

Ernestine and Zach

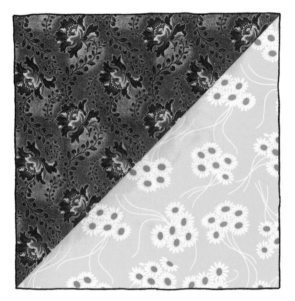

Together in pairs,
they make
eight squares.

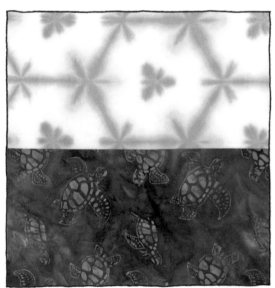

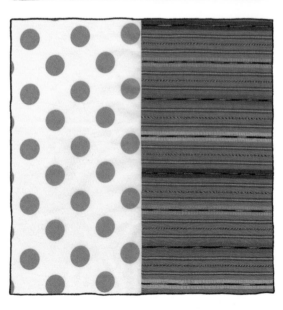

Except for Naika.
Naika works on one blue square.
She uses special pens and paints and brushes.

Next they arrange the squares. They turn them and move them, this way and that.

There are so many combinations.

The last one they try is their favorite.

The rotary blade rolls and cuts fabric along the ruler's edge.

Heavy plastic ruler for measuring and cutting

A rubber mat protects the table.

This quilt will have
a border around four
sides. Jocelyn measures,
and Anna May cuts four
white rectangles. The
pieces look plain, but
not for long!

Anna helps Jennifer cover the palm of her hand with paint.

Jennifer presses her hand onto the fabric.
Friends are invited to make handprints, too.

Now all the pieces are ready.

Labels show which piece goes where.

They pin and sew and iron all the
pieces together. Soon the patchwork
is complete.

Now it is time to layer the quilt.

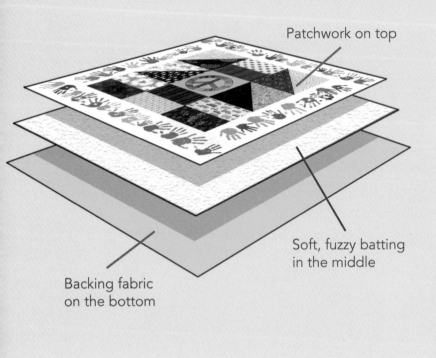

Patchwork on top

Soft, fuzzy batting in the middle

Backing fabric on the bottom

The layers are held in place with basting stitches.

The quilt is attached to wooden rods.

It's rolled tight and stretched across sawhorses.

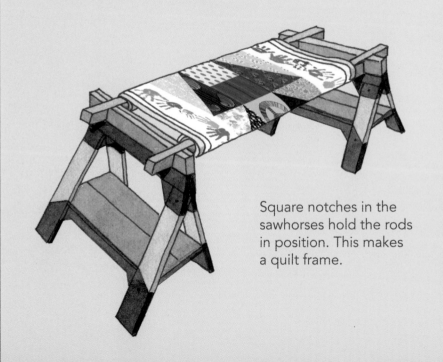

Square notches in the sawhorses hold the rods in position. This makes a quilt frame.

At the frame, Sanaa learns to stitch.
She pokes the needle down from the top
and back up from below. It is hard to find
the right spot! She practices and learns.

It takes a long time to quilt the quilt.
Everybody lends a hand.

On many, many Fridays, they sit and stitch and talk together.

Finally the last stitch is stitched!

The quilt is taken off the frame.

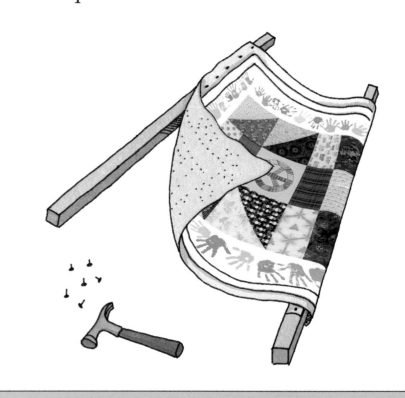

It is trimmed into a neat square.

Dot sews on a purple binding to close the edges.

Many hands worked together to make this beautiful quilt.
But who will have it now that it is done?

Everyone will have it!
It hangs in the library for all to see.

It's the quilt that Jennifer
and her friends made,
all together.

Peace by Piece: The Norwalk Community Quilt Project

This story is based on my real life. I have been making community quilts with friends since 2008 in a group we call Peace by Piece. We gather at the Senior Court Housing Complex in Norwalk, Connecticut. On most Monday and Friday afternoons, senior citizens who live in the apartments, other adult volunteers, and kids living in the neighborhood come together to work on quilts. The word has spread, and friends and grandkids and cousins also join us when they can.

Over the years, thousands of people have sat at the frame and stitched with us at public quilting bees in the community. Our quilts hang in Norwalk public libraries, Newfield Public Library in Bridgeport, Norwalk Community College, and Stepping Stones Museum for Children. It's been a beautiful part of my life, and I am so happy to share our story with you.

A community quilt is a metaphor, showing that good things happen when many come together as one. Thank you to the Norwalk Children's Foundation, Norwalk Housing Authority, Denyse Schmidt Quilts, 22 Haviland Street Gallery, Christie's Quilting Boutique, and our generous donors. Thank you to my early readers/fellow writers: Nina, Katie, and Jan. Thank you to my supportive family and friends, especially my husband, Ken. Thank you to my editor, Nancy Siscoe, and art director Sarah Hokanson at Random House for bringing this story to light!

And most of all, thank you to the quilters of Peace by Piece, past, present, and future. I love you all.

—Lizzy Rockwell

To learn more about Peace by Piece and how to make a quilt, go to thealltogetherquilt.com.
Other good websites: kidsquilt.org and thesprucecrafts.com/quilting-4162899.

Classic Quilt Blocks

A quilt block is made of smaller patches, sewn together. Here are nine classic quilt blocks that use squares, triangles, and rectangles. The possibilities are endless! Try cutting out these shapes in construction paper and then experiment with your own quilt designs. You can make bigger patterns by putting finished blocks next to each other.

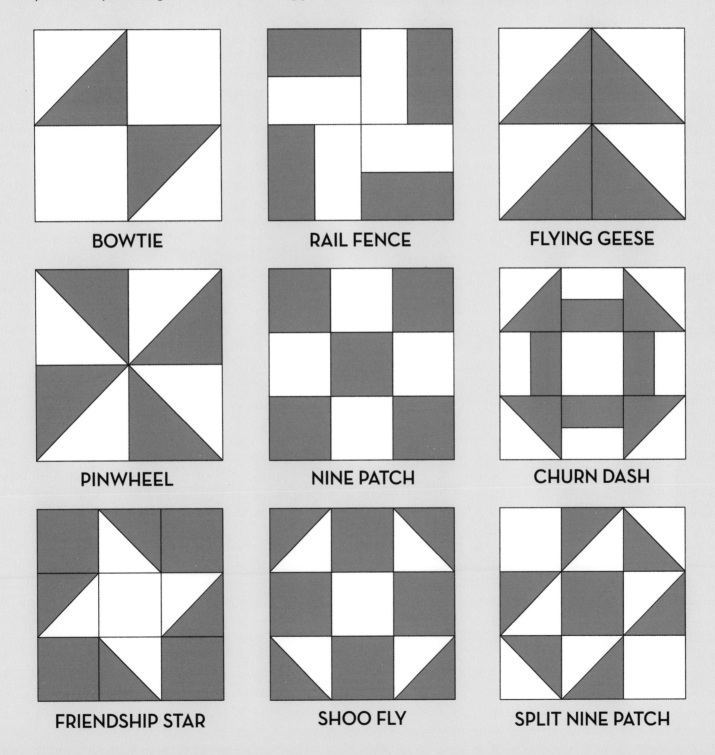

BOWTIE

RAIL FENCE

FLYING GEESE

PINWHEEL

NINE PATCH

CHURN DASH

FRIENDSHIP STAR

SHOO FLY

SPLIT NINE PATCH

About the Quilt

I made the quilt you see in this book. The Peace by Piece quilters, friends, and family helped me with the handprints and the hand-quilting. The peace sign square in the center of the quilt was hand-drawn by Jocelyn Bacila Chara when she was twelve years old. Quilters love to discover, swap, and share their fabrics. Here's the story of the fabrics I chose.

 INDIAN PAISLEY: The paisley teardrop shape is a popular motif all over the world. This fabric was hand-printed in India using carved woodblocks.

 WINTER SPIRITS: Designed by Faye Oliver, an Australian Aboriginal artist. The image depicts ancient spirits watching over creatures at the beginning of the universe.

 TOILE: Toile was popularized in France in the 1700s. This fabric shows scenes of children in the garden. Toile is usually printed in one color on a pale background.

 JAPANESE BUNNIES: This charming bunny pattern would be a popular fabric for an informal cotton kimono, called a yukata. The rabbit is a symbol of cleverness.

 SHIBORI: Shibori is a Japanese handcraft in which the artist twists, folds, and ties sections of fabric with string and then dips those sections in colored dyes to create patterns.

 SHWESHWE: Made in South Africa at the Da Gama Textile Company. Blue indigo fabric is printed with a special acid that bleaches out the white areas.

 DENYSE SCHMIDT BIG DOT: Denyse is a fabric and quilt designer, author, teacher, and friend of mine. Here she took a classic dot pattern and made choices about color, size, and layout.

 MEXICAN MAYAN STRIPE: This pattern is made by hand-weaving colored threads together on a loom. To make a stripe, the up-and-down threads are one color. The side-to-side threads change.

 DENYSE SCHMIDT BIG DAISY: For this pattern, Denyse was inspired by floral designs on American feed sacks from the 1930s.

 SCOTTISH PLAID: To make plaid, different-colored threads are used both going up and down and side to side. When the threads cross, they make patterns.

 FLORAL STRIPE: This fabric was deep in my fabric drawer. I don't know where it came from! It reminds me of cheerful wallpaper in an old farmhouse.

 WILLIAM MORRIS FLORAL: Designed by an English artist named William Morris in 1884. Morris loved natural shapes and colors.

 CARS AND TRUCKS: I bought this novelty fabric in Kyoto, Japan. Novelty fabrics depict objects or creatures, which can have special meaning to the person making or receiving the quilt.

 AFRICAN WAX PRINT: My quilter friend Anne gave me this fabric. She bought it in Mali when she was in the Peace Corps.

 INDONESIAN BATIK: To make a batik pattern, carved wooden stamps are dipped in melted wax and pressed onto fabric. When you dye the fabric, the areas with wax stay white. Then you can remove the wax and dye it again.

 CHINESE GREEN FLORAL: My sister-in-law Keiko bought this fabric for me at an outdoor market in Beijing, China.